Natural Disasters

Hurricanes

Louise Park

A+

Smart Apple Media

Smart Apple Media
2140 Howard Drive West
North Mankato, Minnesota 56003

First published in 2007 by
MACMILLAN EDUCATION AUSTRALIA PTY LTD
627 Chapel Street, South Yarra, Australia 3141

Visit our Web site at www.macmillan.com.au or go directly to www.macmillanlibrary.com.au

Associated companies and representatives throughout the world.

Copyright © Louise Park 2007

Library of Congress Cataloging-in-Publication Data

Park, Louise, 1961-
   Hurricanes / by Louise Park.
   p. cm. – (Natural disasters)
   Includes index.
   ISBN 978-1-59920-112-2
   1. Hurricanes–Juvenile literature. 2. Cyclones–Juvenile literature. 3. Natural disasters–Juvenile
   literature. I. Title.

   QC944.2.P368 2007
   551.55'2–dc22

                                                    2007004658

Edited by Sam Munday and Erin Richards
Text and cover design by Ivan Finnegan, iF design
Page layout by Ivan Finnegan, iF design
Photo research by Jes Senbergs
Illustrations by Andy Craig and Nives Porcellato, pp. 8, 9, 12
Maps by designscope, pp. 6, 10, 16, 20, 26

Printed in U.S.

Acknowledgements

The author and the publisher are grateful to the following for permission to reproduce copyright material:
Front cover photograph: Cyclone Beni hitting Port Vila Bay, Vanuatu Efate Island, January 2003, courtesy of Alamy.

Background textures courtesy of Ivan Finnegan, iF design.

AFP/Getty Images, p. 18; Alamy, pp. 1, 14; Jocelyn Augustino/FEMA, p. 11; Bettmann/Corbis, pp. 20, 21; Andrea Booher/FEMA, p. 10; FairfaxPhotos/Robert Rough, p. 29; FairfaxPhotos/Andrew Taylor, p. 5; Jeff Greenberg/Alamy, p. 24; Susan Greenwood/Getty Images, p. 25; Nicholas Kamm/Getty Images, p. 28; La Tribuna/MSF, p. 17; Dr Richard Legeckis/Science Photo Library, p. 7; NASA, p. 4; NASA/Goddard Space Flight Center/Science Photo Library, p. 16; National Library of Australia, p. 27; NOAA, pp. 13, 15, 19; Northern Territory Library/Lorna Laffer Collection, p. 26; Photolibrary, p. 22.

While every care has been taken to trace and acknowledge copyright, the publisher tenders their apologies for any accidental infringement where copyright has proved untraceable. Where the attempt has been unsuccessful, the publisher welcomes information that would redress the situation.

Contents

GLOSSARY WORDS
When a word is printed in **bold**, you can look up its meaning in the glossary on page 31.

Natural disasters

Natural disasters are events that occur naturally. They are not caused by human action. They can happen all over the world at any time. When natural disasters occur in populated areas, they can result in death, injury, and damage to property.

Types of natural disasters

There are many types of natural disaster, such as tornadoes, wildfires, droughts, and earthquakes. Each type occurs for a very different reason and affects the Earth in different ways. Although they are different, they all create chaos and bring **devastation** and destruction with them wherever they strike.

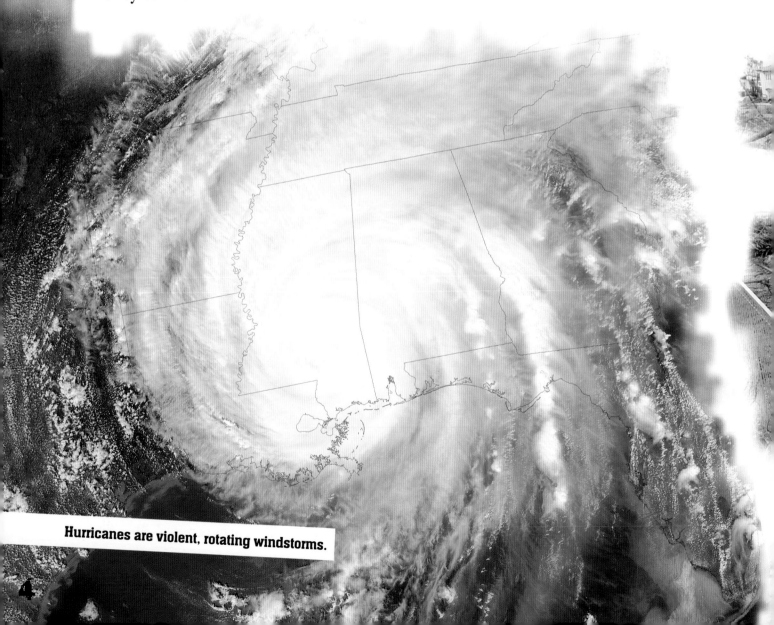

Hurricanes are violent, rotating windstorms.

Hurricanes

Hurricanes are revolving windstorms that are much more powerful than ordinary storms. They have winds that whirl around at high speeds in a circular motion. Powerful hurricanes can be very destructive and are one of the world's recurring natural disasters.

What is a hurricane?

A hurricane is a large spinning mass of wind. It has rotating winds that can reach speeds of over 75 miles (120 km) an hour or more. These winds spiral upwards and rotate faster and faster, forming a huge circle that can be up to 1,240 miles (2,000 km) wide. In the center of a hurricane is a calm area known as the **eye** of the storm.

DID YOU KNOW?
Hurricanes have different names depending on what part of the world they occur in. They can be called hurricanes, typhoons, or cyclones.

On March 20, 2006, Cyclone Larry hit the coast of Queensland, Australia.

Where hurricanes occur

Strong hurricane-type winds can occur anywhere in the world, but true hurricanes only form over oceans in **tropical regions**. Hurricanes have different names depending on the oceans that they form above. Hurricanes that occur over the Atlantic Ocean are called hurricanes. When they form over the Indian Ocean, they are called cyclones. Hurricanes that build over the Pacific Ocean are known as typhoons. Hurricanes, cyclones, and typhoons develop over warm seas near the **Equator**.

Hurricane zones

Hurricane zones lie in tropical areas near the Equator. Some of the world's hottest locations are found along the Equator. The sea is very warm in these areas, with temperatures rarely below 79 °F (26 °C). These very warm seas create ideal conditions for hurricanes to form. The areas where the seas are warm like this are known as hurricane zones.

All hurricanes begin over the ocean and most of them develop in hurricane zones.

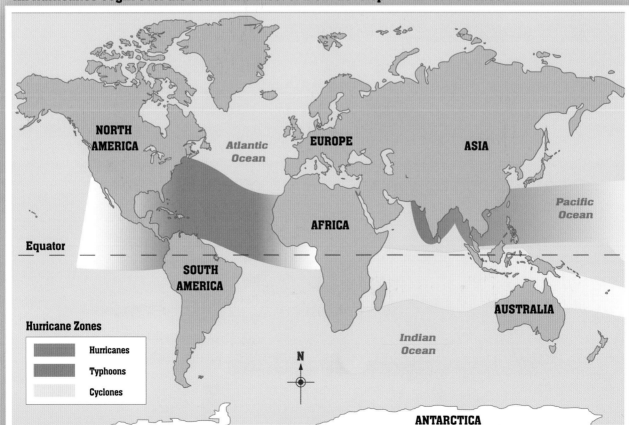

NORTH AMERICA

Atlantic Ocean

EUROPE

ASIA

Pacific Ocean

AFRICA

Equator

SOUTH AMERICA

AUSTRALIA

Indian Ocean

N

Hurricane Zones

- Hurricanes
- Typhoons
- Cyclones

ANTARCTICA

The Equator

The Equator is the perfect place for hurricanes to start because it is so hot. The heat causes huge masses of air and moisture to move and rise. It is during this air movement that a hurricane can be created.

The sun's rays reach different places on Earth at different angles. Different angles deliver different amounts of heat. At the Equator, the sun's rays are almost directly overhead. This means that there is more heat here than anywhere else on Earth.

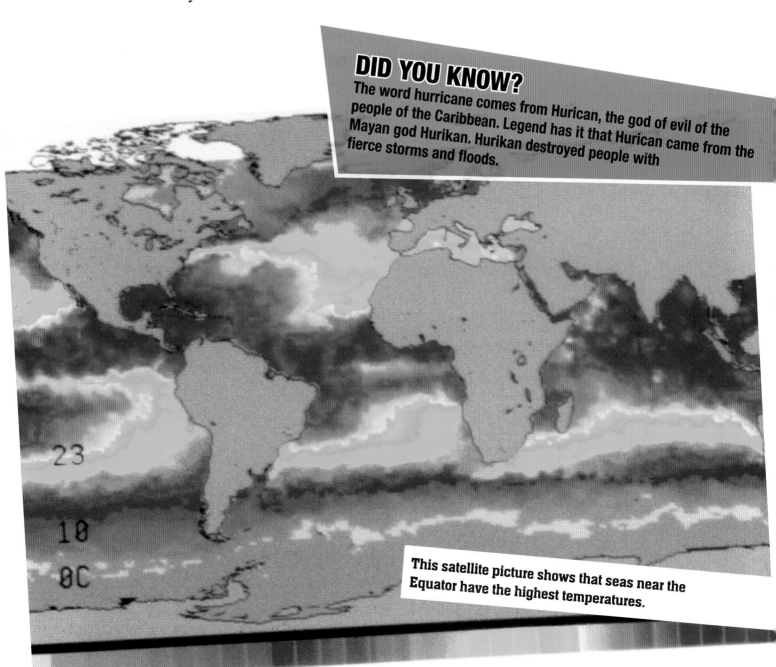

DID YOU KNOW?
The word hurricane comes from Hurican, the god of evil of the people of the Caribbean. Legend has it that Hurican came from the Mayan god Hurikan. Hurikan destroyed people with fierce storms and floods.

This satellite picture shows that seas near the Equator have the highest temperatures.

Hurricane formation

Hurricanes form from heavy thunderclouds filled with water droplets. When these thunderclouds combine with fast winds, conditions are right for a hurricane to form.

The water cycle

Thunderclouds are created as part of Earth's natural water cycle. As the sun and warm air heat Earth, water **evaporates** into **water vapor**. Water vapor is an invisible gas that rises up into the **atmosphere.** As the vapor rises, it cools, collects, and **condenses** into water droplets to form clouds. When large thunderclouds join together, they can unleash enormous amounts of rain. If these clouds develop into a hurricane, this rain often causes damage.

Think about it

In tropical areas, the water cycle can be extreme because the sun is so powerful. Warm air that rises quickly in tropical areas draws enormous amounts of water vapor with it. The clouds that form here can create massive thunderstorms. When these massive thunderstorms join together, a hurricane can form.

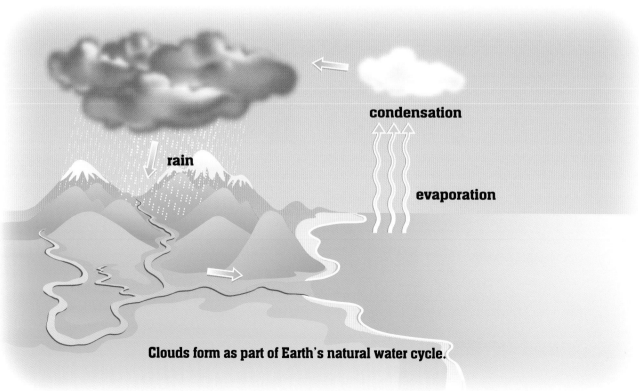

condensation

rain

evaporation

Clouds form as part of Earth's natural water cycle.

Wind

Wind is caused by air moving from cool, dry areas and warm, **humid** areas. These areas are known as **high pressure areas** and **low pressure areas**. When warm, humid air rises from a low pressure area it causes cooler, high pressure air to rush in and fill the space. When the exchange of air is small, it can create a gentle breeze. When a large amount of low pressure air pulls upward from the Earth, it creates an updraft. When this happens, a downdraft of high pressure air rushes rapidly into the space. This large exchange of air gives the wind its speed. If enough air is moved quickly enough, the spiraling winds being sucked up can create a hurricane.

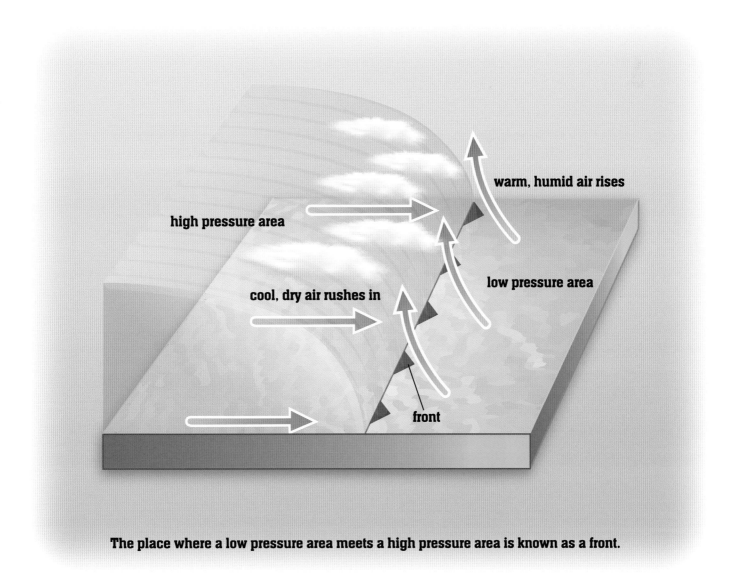

warm, humid air rises

high pressure area

low pressure area

cool, dry air rushes in

front

The place where a low pressure area meets a high pressure area is known as a front.

ISASTER FILE
urricane Katrina

HAT	The most expensive hurricane in the history of the United States
HERE	The Bahamas and most of eastern North America, especially greater New Orleans
VHEN	August 23–31, 2005
CATEGORY	5

Hurricane Katrina formed over the Bahamas and was just a category one hurricane when it crossed into Florida. From there, it hit the Gulf of Mexico where it became one of the strongest hurricanes ever recorded in the Gulf. At its strongest, Hurricane Katrina's winds were recorded at around 174 miles (280 km) an hour. Warnings had not been issued because forecasters had not expected the hurricane to gain so much strength.

Hurricane Katrina devastated much of New Orleans.

Why did it happen?

Hurricane Katrina first formed as a **tropical depression**. It became a hurricane just two hours before it hit the coast. When the storm moved into the Gulf, it became more powerful. This occurred because it moved over a very warm area. Katrina grew in size and strength as warm, moist air was sucked in.

Counting the cost

The hurricane created huge waves that flooded the city of New Orleans. It is estimated that 1,605 people were killed, with most of the deaths occurring in Louisiana.

Damage from Hurricane Katrina created a massive refugee problem, with people who had lost their homes needing to be relocated. The majority of refugees were taken to Texas, with over 230,000 people taking shelter in Houston. More than 58,000 members of the National Guard were brought in to deal with Katrina's aftermath. These troops came from every state in the U.S.

Troops search for survivors in Katrina's aftermath.

DID YOU KNOW?
Hurricanes do the most damag[e]
first 12 hours once they hit la[nd]

How hurricanes begin

Hurricanes usually begin where winds meet over very warm seas with temperatures of around 79°F (26°C). Masses of warm, moist air rise up in a spinning motion, creating an area of low pressure. More air rushes into the space created and the whirling builds. As the warm air rises and cools, the moisture within it condenses. This condensation forms large thunderclouds. When these large thunderstorms grow, they join with others and form a tropical depression.

The air moving inside the storm gathers speed, creating a **tropical storm**. If the tropical storm continues to gather speed, it becomes a hurricane. Winds in tropical storms move at speeds of 39-74 miles (63-119 km) an hour. Winds in a hurricane can reach over 124 miles (200 km) an hour.

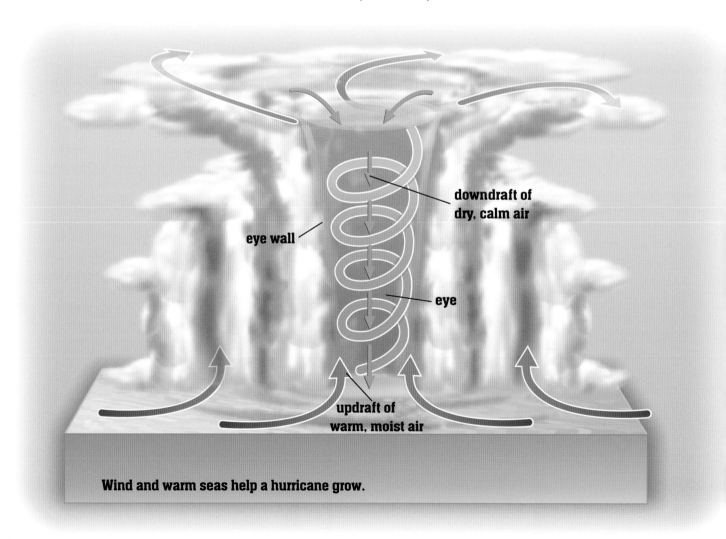

downdraft of dry, calm air

eye wall

eye

updraft of warm, moist air

Wind and warm seas help a hurricane grow.

The eye of a hurricane

The eye of the hurricane is a wide column of dry, calm air in the middle of the whirling winds. It descends from clear sky to the ground. The whirling air and clouds continue to spin around it and gather speed. This eventually forms the hurricane.

The strongest winds are found immediately around the eye of a hurricane. This area is known as the "eye wall." It is here that the whirling winds can reach over 124 miles (200 km) an hour.

DID YOU KNOW?
The eye of a hurricane can be between 19–62 miles (30–100 km) wide.

Winds pick up speed as they spin tightly around the eye of the storm.

How hurricanes move

Hurricanes move in two ways. They spin inside themselves and they move over Earth.

What helps a hurricane spin?

The rotation of Earth helps a hurricane spin. As Earth spins on its axis, the air in the atmosphere moves with it. This creates winds that veer to the north in the Northern Hemisphere and to the south in the Southern Hemisphere. Therefore, air is already moving in a particular direction when a hurricane begins to build. As more and more air is sucked in, the winds gather more and more speed and swirl in the same direction. Hurricanes spin counterclockwise in the Northern Hemisphere and clockwise in the Southern Hemisphere.

When a hurricane reaches land, it can cause severe damage.

On the move

Winds blowing outside the hurricane move it along. A hurricane can travel at speeds of up to 19 miles (30 km) an hour. As long as the hurricane can draw in moist, warm air it will continue to grow and move. As it travels across the ocean, the sea provides very little resistance to it and helps fuel it.

Where a hurricane travels

A hurricane travels across the ocean, getting faster as it goes. Not all hurricanes travel in a predictable way. Most move backward and forward making it very hard to predict what the hurricane will do. Some reach **landfall** very quickly. Others will move around and may not strike land at all.

When a hurricane moves over land, it starts to run out of fuel. This is because it cannot pick up warm moisture from the sea to feed it. There is also more friction over land as the hurricane hits **vegetation**, buildings, and other objects. This friction starts to slow the winds down until the hurricane eventually stops.

When Hurricane Hugo hit land in Puerto Rico in 1989, buildings were destroyed, roofs lifted, and 50,000 people were left homeless.

DISASTER FILE

Hurricane Mitch

WHAT	One of the most powerful hurricanes ever recorded
WHERE	Honduras, Nicaragua, El Salvador, and south Florida
WHEN	October 2–November 5, 1998
CATEGORY	5

Hurricane Mitch developed over the Caribbean Sea. It became one of the strongest Atlantic hurricanes ever recorded. Hurricane Mitch hovered over water for many days before moving toward land. By the time Mitch reached landfall it had weakened. Its winds, recorded at an incredible 180 miles (290 km) per hour, had dropped back down. However, extreme damage was caused by the massive rainfalls that Mitch created.

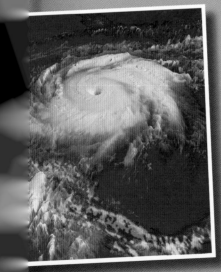

This satellite image shows Hurricane Mitch approaching Central America.

Why did it happen?

Hurricane Mitch developed from weather changes over western Africa known as tropical waves. Tropical depressions can form when cloud mass from these waves grows and starts to rotate.

The reason Mitch produced enormous amounts of rainfall was partly due to the mountains in Central America. The combination of volcanic peaks and Mitch's slow movement led to a total rainfall measurement of 75 inches (190.5 cm). These rains were responsible for the devastating floods and mud slides.

Counting the cost

Though Mitch had weakened as it hit land, it still caused massive damage. It dropped huge amounts of rainfall over the coast of Central America, causing floods. Deaths as a result of this flooding are thought to be around 11,000. At the end of 1998, over 8,000 people were still reported missing.

Hurricane Mitch caused extreme devastation to towns, villages, homes, crops, and farmland. The ongoing costs of this devastation are yet to be calculated. Initial damages were recorded at $7 billion. The areas affected by Hurricane Mitch will take decades to recover.

Hurricane Mitch caused extreme flooding and damage in Central America.

Think about it

Mitch caused over 800,000 people to flee their homes. Seventy percent of the crops in the country of Honduras were destroyed and farmland was ruined.

When hurricanes hit

When hurricanes hit land, they bring destruction and devastation with them. The worst disasters occur in coastal areas because they are the first places to be hit. There are three main ways that a hurricane can cause destruction: storm surges, wind, and rain.

Storm surges

Storm surges are enormous walls of seawater that are driven toward the shore. The power of a hurricane can be so great that it can create waves up to 26 feet (8 m) high. The sea level also rises. The combination of this and the enormous waves brings flooding which can destroy low-lying coastal areas.

DID YOU KNOW?
Many things can affect the level of a storm surge:
• the slope of the seafloor as it approaches land
• the speed of the storm
• how low the air pressure is at the center of the eye
—the lower the air pressure the stronger the surge

In April 1991, a cyclone that formed in the Bay of Bengal hit Bangladesh with storm surges over 23 feet (7 m) high.

Wind

The most obvious cause of destruction from a hurricane is wind. The whirling winds of a hurricane can cause significant damage. They can be powerful enough to rip trees out of the ground, upturn trucks, and lift buildings.

Rain

As the wind is sucked up into a hurricane, it can pull large amounts of seawater with it. As the thunderstorms join together, vast amounts of rain are produced. Even without a storm surge, the rain from a hurricane can be **torrential**. More rain can fall from a hurricane in one day than would normally fall in a year. Rain can cause flooding and can also mix with soil to create mudslides.

Hurricane Andrew hit the U.S. in 1992, with strong winds that ripped roofs and walls off buildings.

DISASTER FILE
Typhoon Vera

WHAT	The strongest typhoon to hit Japan in recorded history
WHERE	Japan
WHEN	September 21–28, 1959
CATEGORY	5

When Typhoon Vera slammed into the southern coast of Japan, its winds were measured at 160 miles (257 km) an hour. Typhoon Vera was given the name "super typhoon." Vera was most devastating because it brought all the destructive elements of a hurricane with it. Japan was hit with storm surges, extremely powerful winds, and torrential rain. It caused widespread damage and flooding.

Why did it happen?

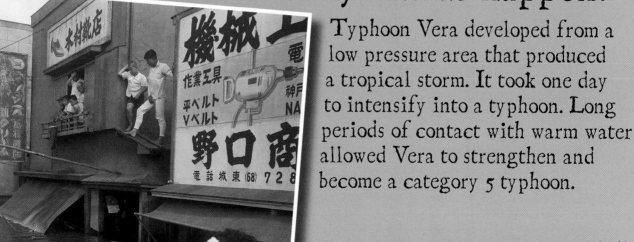

Typhoon Vera developed from a low pressure area that produced a tropical storm. It took one day to intensify into a typhoon. Long periods of contact with warm water allowed Vera to strengthen and become a category 5 typhoon.

The combination of storm surges and torrential rain caused widespread flooding in southern Japan.

Counting the cost

Typhoon Vera was one of Japan's worst natural disasters. It destroyed sea walls, roads, homes, and large crop areas. This super typhoon took the lives of 5,238 people. Almost 1.6 million people were left homeless and over 32,000 people were injured.

Typhoon Vera produced massive storm surges that slammed into the coast of Japan.

Think about it

Many typhoons hit Japan between June and October. However, August and September are generally the worst months for tropical storms. As typhoons approach Japan, they lose their strength because the waters around the country are cooler than in the tropics. By the time they get close, most typhoons turn into tropical storms.

Studying hurricanes

Meteorologists are scientists who study and predict the weather. Because hurricanes occur mostly in hurricane zones, it is usually quite easy to predict where a hurricane is going to form. It is much harder to predict if and where a hurricane will reach landfall and do damage. When conditions are right for hurricanes to build, the hurricane season begins. Meteorologists use information gathered by satellites, radar, and other tools to watch the weather closely during the hurricane season.

Satellites

Satellites gather useful information that meteorologists rely on to do their job. Satellites sit outside Earth's atmosphere and collect information about temperatures and weather patterns. Maps are produced as a result of this information. Meteorologists study these maps carefully to assess the situation.

Meteorologists study weather patterns to determine if a hurricane will develop.

Dppler radars

Doppler radars show the directions and speeds of the winds blowing in and around a hurricane. Doppler radars send out radio waves from an antenna. Objects in the air, such as raindrops, hailstones, insects, or dust, reflect some of the radio waves back to the antenna. This information is converted from radio waves into pictures that show what is happening in the cloud circulation. Meteorologists use these pictures to understand what is happening and what is likely to happen in the following hours.

Measuring hurricanes on a scale

The Saffir-Simpson Hurricane Scale is used to classify hurricanes into categories. Meteorologists study a hurricane and assess its wind strength. They then try to predict how high the storm surge will be and the potential damage from it. They use this information to grade the hurricane from one to five on the scale.

SAFFIR-SIMPSON HURRICANE SCALE

Category	Wind speed	Storm surge	Potential damage	Description
1	74–95 miles (119–153 km) an hour	4–5 feet (1.2–1.5 m)	minimal	• damage primarily to vegetation • some coastal flooding
2	96–110 miles (154–177 km) an hour	6–8 feet (1.8–2.4 m)	moderate	• tiles blown off roofs • broken windows • coastal flooding
3	111–130 miles (178–209 km) an hour	9–12 feet (2.7–3.7 m)	severe	• structural damage to buildings • mobile homes destroyed • flooding and floating debris damage coastal buildings
4	131–155 miles (210–249 km) an hour	13–18 feet (4–5.5 m)	extreme	• extensive structural damage to buildings, including complete roof failure • severe flooding extends inland
5	155+ miles (250+ km) an hour	18+ feet (5.5+ m)	catastrophic	• complete roof failure to many buildings • many structures completely blown over • major flood damage to coastal buildings • mass evacuation required

Hurricane warning

Warning people that a hurricane is on its way is the best way to prevent loss of lives. Meteorologists are under great pressure to predict the strength of a hurricane and where it will hit. When meteorologists announce a hurricane watch, this alerts people that a hurricane could hit within the next 36 hours. When meteorologists predict that the hurricane could hit within 24 hours, they issue a hurricane warning.

A hurricane warning is broadcast on television, radio, and through all forms of the media to reach the biggest audience possible. Evacuations begin when the hurricane is about 12–18 hours away. Around this time, radar information helps meteorologists predict more accurately where a hurricane will reach landfall.

Meteorologists examine information to help them make the most accurate predictions possible.

Preparing for a hurricane

There is much that can be done to prepare for a hurricane. Objects that can be thrown by a hurricane need to be secured or packed away. All kinds of everyday items can become dangerous during a hurricane. Bikes, chairs, bins, and even cars can be thrown miles from where they originally were. Some "at risk" communities may have emergency plans, evacuation routes, and emergency shelters already prepared.

DID YOU KNOW?

In harbors and marinas, people warn that a hurricane is coming by using flags. They hoist two red flags with black squares in their centers up on flagpoles. They are marine hurricane warning flags. Sailors recognize these flags and know that a hurricane is about to hit.

Hurricane warning flags are one way of alerting people to prepare for a hurricane.

ISASTER FILE

yclone Tracy

WHAT	The most destructive cyclone ever to hit an Australian community
WHERE	Darwin, Australia
WHEN	December 21–26, 1974
CATEGORY	4

For most of its journey, Cyclone Tracy did not appear to be a major threat to the city of Darwin. But on the morning of Christmas Eve, it changed direction and rounded the tip of Bathurst Island, north of Darwin. This meant it was heading straight for Darwin. From around midnight to 7 A.M. on Christmas Day, Cyclone Tracy passed over Darwin. It brought torrential rainfall as well as strong winds recorded at 135 miles (217 km) an hour.

Why did it happen?

Cyclone Tracy developed from a tropical depression in the Arafura Sea. This depression gained wind strength over 24 hours. When winds reached over 39 miles (63 km) an hour, the tropical storm was named Tracy.

The city of Darwin was not prepared for the strong winds of Cyclone Tracy.

Counting the cost

Darwin disintegrated under the impact of winds of over 135 miles (217 km) an hour. Houses and buildings collapsed, because they had not been built to withstand such strong winds. Darwin also suffered from huge torrential rains. At the time, Darwin had approximately 48,000 residents. More than 25,000 had to be evacuated and at least 20,000 people were left homeless. Approximately 70 percent of Darwin's homes were destroyed. Darwin lost all its services due to damage. There was no power, water, or sewerage. Cyclone Tracy also claimed the lives of 71 people.

Cyclone Tracy caused so much damage that the city of Darwin had to be rebuilt.

Disaster relief

The problems created by hurricanes do not stop once the storm has passed. Severe tropical storms cause devastation to land and property. Water is often contaminated and many vital services can be cut off. Sickness and disease can be a big problem after a hurricane.

Rescue and relief

After a hurricane has struck, there is much to be done. The first step is to rescue any survivors. Often people can be trapped by floods or caught among the damage. Areas are set up where relief can be provided to victims. People may need more than medical attention. They might need dry clothing and shelter, food, and fresh water.

After relief efforts have been established workers can assess the damage and begin cleaning up. Often people have to start all over again. Dangerously damaged structures need to be demolished. Once the area has been cleared, rebuilding can begin.

Rescue workers pick their way through the debris.

Rebuilding

Once survivors have been rescued and people provided for, then the rebuilding begins. Any buildings ruled unsafe must be demolished. Then the **debris** needs to be cleared. Power lines, gas pipes, and drains all need to be examined. If the damage is very bad, rebuilding can take years. For some communities, such as Darwin, rebuilding is an opportunity for improvement. Darwin's buildings were not built to withstand cyclones. After Cyclone Tracy, new building codes were introduced. Rebuilding Darwin has meant a safer city for all of its residents.

In poorer countries, hurricanes often cause food shortages due to damage to crops and farmland. When hurricanes hit poorer countries, global aid is very important. These countries need financial assistance for a long time so that they can fully recover.

Hurricanes can destroy whole crops and cause food shortages.

DISASTER FILES AT A GLANCE

The four severe tropical storms profiled in this book are record-breaking for different reasons. This graph shows their size and their death tolls.

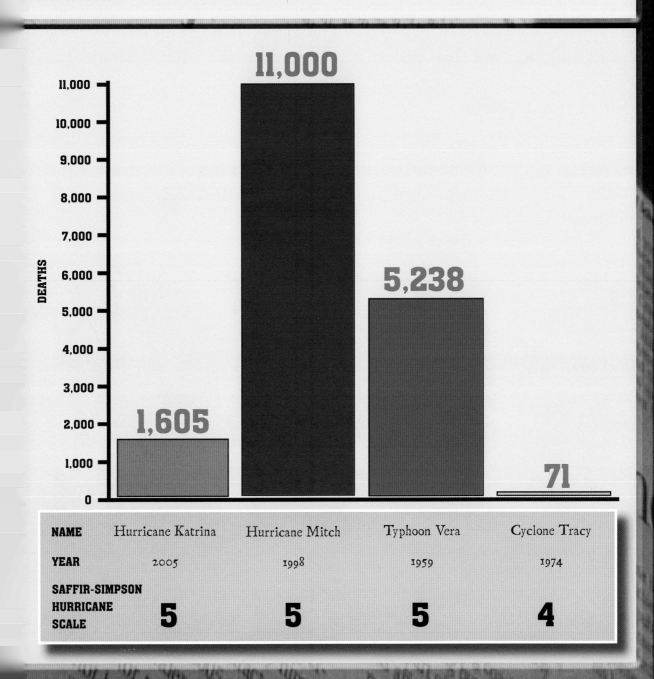

NAME	Hurricane Katrina	Hurricane Mitch	Typhoon Vera	Cyclone Tracy
YEAR	2005	1998	1959	1974
SAFFIR-SIMPSON HURRICANE SCALE	5	5	5	4

Glossary

atmosphere	blanket of gases that surrounds Earth
condenses	when gas changes into liquid
debris	the remains of things that have been broken or destroyed
devastation	severe damage or destruction
Equator	imaginary line around Earth's middle
evaporates	when liquid changes into gas
eye	low pressure center of a hurricane, with calm winds
high pressure areas	large areas of cool, dry air
humid	contains a lot of water or water vapor
landfall	when a hurricane moves across the ocean and reaches land
low pressure areas	large areas of warm, humid air
torrential	pouring down in great amounts
tropical depression	tropical weather system with winds of less than 39 miles (63 km) an hour
tropical storm	tropical weather system with winds between 39 and 74 miles (63 and 119 km) an hour
tropical regions	hot and humid areas on either side of the Equator
vegetation	the plants of an area
water vapor	water as a gas

Index